WILD ONES
GIRAFFES

by JILL ANDERSON

NorthWord
Minnetonka, Minnesota

It is morning on the plains of Africa.

Two very unusual animals stand in the distance.

It is a mother giraffe and her baby.

She is called
a cow. Her baby
is a calf.
Here and there,
other giraffes graze quietly.

Look
at
their
l-o-o-o-ong
necks!

They have
very long
legs, too.
They stand
on hard feet
called hooves,
which can
be as big as
a dinner plate.

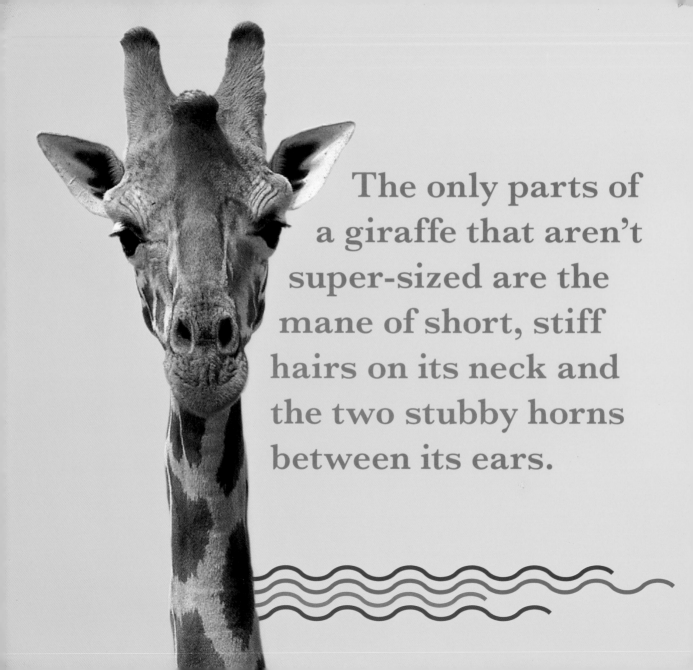

The only parts of a giraffe that aren't super-sized are the mane of short, stiff hairs on its neck and the two stubby horns between its ears.

With such a long neck, the giraffe is built to be a leaf eater. It can reach treetops that no other animal can reach.

Its long, black tongue rips the leaves off the branches.

It is much harder for a giraffe to reach the ground. It must spread its front legs apart and

s-t-r-e-t-c-h

its neck just to get a drink of water.

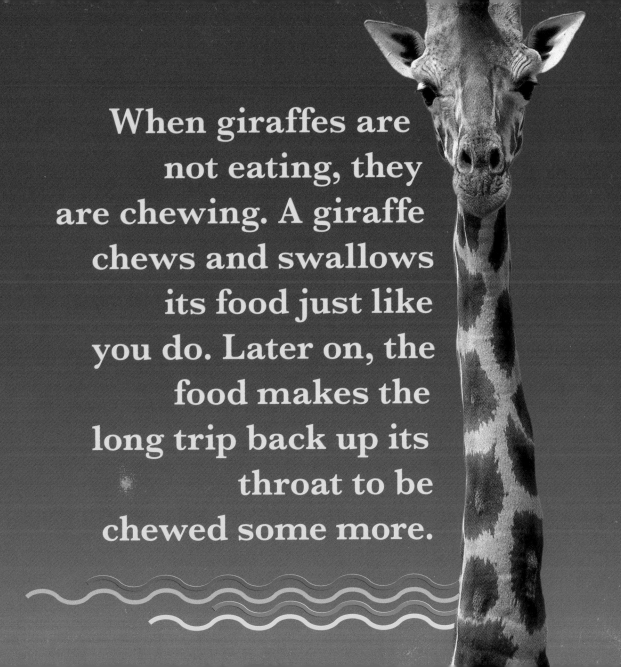

When giraffes are not eating, they are chewing. A giraffe chews and swallows its food just like you do. Later on, the food makes the long trip back up its throat to be chewed some more.

When a calf is first born, its body isn't ready to nibble on leaves. grow **big** and **strong.** It needs its mother's milk to This can be a real stretch for a small calf!

When the calf is a little older,
it plays around with other calves.
They chase and push each other
to see who's strongest. Their
mothers take turns babysitting.

If a mother giraffe senses danger, she tucks her baby underneath her.

One kick with her sharp hooves may kill a lion that gets too close.

As the sun sets, the giraffes' spotted coats blend in with the shadows.

Standing tall, they will rest until tomorrow comes.

For Alastriona,
the first baby I fell in love with
—J. A.

Composed in the United States of America
Designed by Lois A. Rainwater • Edited by Kristen McCurry

Text © 2005 by Jill Anderson

NORTHWORD
Books for Young Readers
11571 K-Tel Drive
Minnetonka, MN 55343
www.tnkidsbooks.com

Photographs © 2005 provided by:
Anup & Manoj Shah: cover, pp. 14, 18; Digital Vision/Punchstock.com: back cover, pp. 1, 9, 13, 19, 21;
Robin Brandt: endsheets, pp. 2-3; Brand X Pictures/Punchstock.com: pp. 5, 20;
Frans Lanting/2003 Minden Pictures: p. 6; Craig Brandt: pp. 7, 8, 15, 24;
Mitsuaki Iwago/2003 Minden Pictures: pp. 10-11; Garykramer.net: p. 12;
YVA Momatiuk/John Eastcott/Minden Pictures: p. 16; Photodisc/Punchstock.com: pp. 22-23.

Library of Congress Cataloging-in-Publication Data

Anderson, Jill.
Giraffes / by Jill Anderson.
p. cm. -- (Wild ones)
ISBN 1-55971-928-1 (hardcover) -- ISBN 1-55971-929-X (pbk.)
1. Giraffe--Juvenile literature. I. Title. II. Series.

QL737.U56A535 2005

599.638--dc22   2004031117

Printed in Malaysia
10 9 8 7 6 5 4 3 2 1

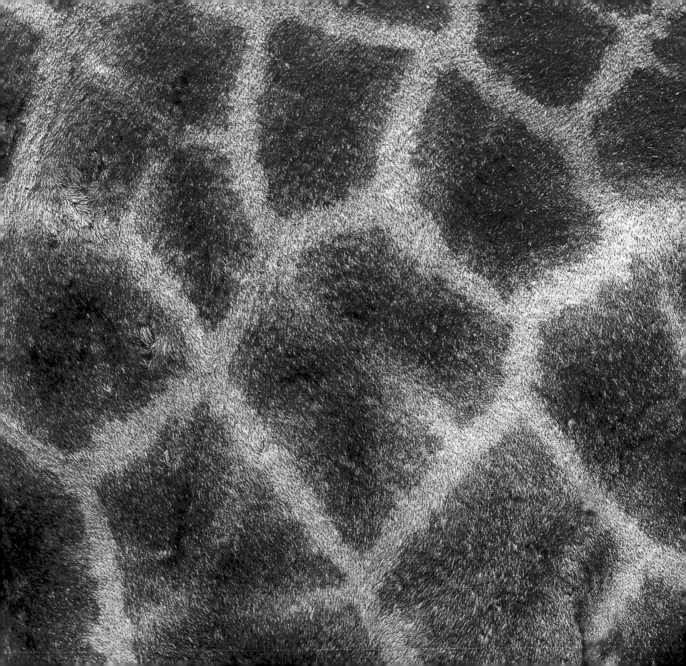